Introduction

The prayers in this book were especially written for children. They guide children toward answers to questions about their relationship with God. Each simple prayer helps them talk to God about their problems. These prayers also help children understand lessons that the Bible teaches. Every prayer follows the topic of a matching story from The Beginners Bible™ "First Book of Bible Stories-Catholic Edition."

THE REGINA PRESS
10 Hub Drive
Melville, NY 11747

International Standard Book Number: 0-88271-564-X

Don Wise, Producer
Randy White, Production Manager
Performance Unlimited, Inc.
1710 General George Patton Drive, Suite 110
Brentwood, Tennessee 37027

First Book of
Prayers

CATHOLIC EDITION

Illustrated by
Kelly R. Pulley
Lisa S. Reed

Regina Press

Table Of Contents

Responsibility (Adam and Eve)   7

Patience (Noah and the Ark)   9

Laughter (Abraham and Sarah)   11

Love (Joseph and His Brothers)   13

Caring (Baby Moses)   15

Fear (Gideon)   17

Determination (Ruth and Naomi)   19

Sadness (Hannah)   21

Respect (Samuel)   23

Wisdom (Solomon)   25

Listening (Elijah)   27

Bravery (Esther)   29

Faith (Daniel)   31

Obedience (Jonah)   33

Helping (The Good Samaritan)   35

Kindness (Jesus and the Children)   37

Forgiveness (Zacchaeus)   39

Happiness (Peter Fills His Net)   41

Teaching (Saul Becomes Paul)   43

Catholic Prayers and Devotions   45

Responsibility

God, it makes me feel good to take care of things that belong to me. When someone lets me borrow something, help me to take care of it and treat it as if it was my own.

Adam and Eve
Genesis 2-3

Patience

Please help me to be patient when I want something. Teach me to wait quietly without complaining. Show me that good things come to those who wait.

Noah and the Ark
Genesis 6-8

Laughter

God, You have shown me that laughing makes people feel good. Please help me to learn to share this good feeling with others so that they can feel good, too.

Abraham and Sarah
Genesis 12-21

Love

God, help me to tell others how much I love them. Teach me to care by giving to others who need help. Show me how to be more thoughtful each day. Please help me to love others the way you love me.

Joseph and His Brothers
Genesis 37

Caring

Please teach me to be more caring and thoughtful to those I love. Help me to remember that you always care for me even when I do something wrong. Thank you for watching over me each day.

Baby Moses
Exodus 1-2

Fear

Thank you, God, for being there for me when I am scared. You always calm my fears. Teach me to be strong and trust that you will keep me safe.

Gideon
Judges 6-7

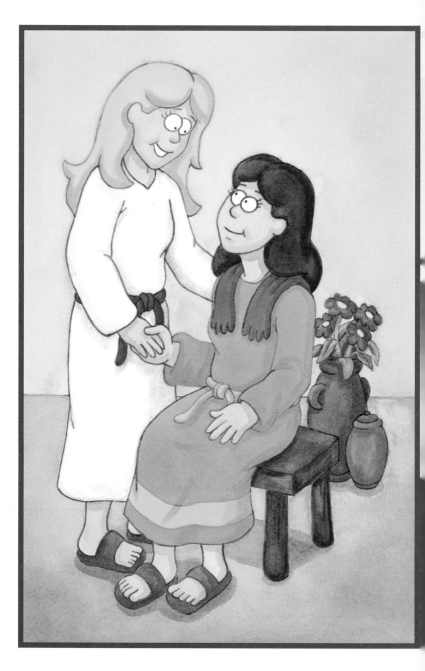

Determination

God, sometimes I get so tired when I am working on a task. Please give me the strength to continue until I am finished. Please teach me to keep trying, because I know that anything is possible with your help.

Ruth and Naomi
Ruth 1-4

Sadness

When I am sad, please teach me to think about happy things. Help me to know that you will take care of everything and you will make me happy again. Show me that time often heals sadness.

Hannah
1 Samuel 1-2

Respect

God, it makes me feel good when people are nice to me. Teach me to respect other people and the choices they make. Help me treat others the way I like to be treated.

Samuel
1 Samuel 3

Wisdom

Please give me wisdom to know right from wrong. Whenever I have a problem, show me what I should do. Help me to remember what I learn so I can teach others.

Solomon
1 Kings 1-4

Listening

Thank you, God, for listening to me when I speak to you. Please teach me to be a good listener. Help me pay attention to others when they are speaking to me.

Elijah
1 Kings 16-17

Bravery

Thank you, God, for giving me the strength to stand up for what I believe is right. Help me to see that my beliefs are important.

Esther
Esther 2-7

Faith

God, I know that I can have faith in you. You have shown me that you want the best for me. I want to make sure you are pleased with me. Help me believe in myself and trust in you.

Daniel
Daniel 6

Obedience

Thank you, God, for my parents and teachers. When someone asks me to do something, please help me do what they say. Help me understand that my parents and teachers know what is best for me.

Jonah
Jonah 1-3

Helping

Sometimes, I meet people who need help. Please show me how to help them. Teach me to see them as equal and treat them with kindness.

The Good Samaritan
Luke 10

Kindness

Thank you, God, for showing your kindness to me every day. Help me to be kind to everyone I meet. Even when people are mean to me, teach me to be good-hearted.

Jesus and the Children
Matthew 19

Forgiveness

When others upset or hurt me, help me to forgive them. Teach me to forgive people when they tell me they are sorry. Help me to remember that you have forgiven me for times when I was bad. So, I should try to forgive others, too.

Zacchaeus
Luke 19

Happiness

God, thank you for my family and friends. I am glad you gave them to me. They make me feel happy when I am sad. Help me stand beside my friends and family during happy times and sad times.

Peter Fills His Net
John 21

Teaching

God, thank you for teaching me about your love. Help me to learn more every day so I can teach others. Teach me to ask questions when there are things I do not understand.

Saul Becomes Paul
Acts 9

CATHOLIC PRAYERS AND DEVOTIONS

The Sign of the Cross

In the name of the Father,
and of the Son,
and of the Holy Spirit. Amen.

Glory Be

Glory be to the Father
and to the Son
and the Holy Spirit,
as it was in the beginning,
is now and ever shall be,
world without end. Amen.

Grace Before Meals

Bless us, O Lord, and these Your gifts
which we are about to receive
from Your bounty
Through Christ our Lord. Amen.

Grace After Meals

We give you thanks, O almighty God,
for all your benefits;
You who live and reign,
world without end. Amen.

The Our Father

Our Father, who art in heaven,
hallowed be Thy name,
Thy kingdom come,
Thy will be done,
on earth as it is in heaven.
Give us this day our daily bread,
and forgive us our trespasses
as we forgive those
who trespass against us,
and lead us not into temptation,
but deliver us from evil. Amen.

The Hail Mary

Hail Mary, full of grace,
the Lord is with thee;
blessed art thou among women,
and blessed is the fruit
of thy womb, Jesus.
Holy Mary, Mother of God,
pray for us sinners now
and at the hour of our death. Amen.

Guardian Angel Prayer

Oh Angel of God
my Guardian dear
to whom God's love
commits me here.
Ever this day
be at my side
to light and guard
to rule and guide.
Amen

The Sacraments

1. Baptism

2. Confirmation

3. Holy Eucharist

4. Reconciliation

5. Anointing of the Sick

6. Holy Orders

7. Matrimony

The Chief Spiritual Works of Mercy

To admonish the sinner.

To instruct the ignorant.

To counsel the doubtful.

To comfort the sorrowful.

To bear wrongs patiently.

To forgive all injuries.

To pray for the living and the dead.

The Chief Corporal Works of Mercy

To feed the hungry.

To give drink to the thirsty.

To clothe the naked.

To visit the imprisoned.

To shelter the homeless.

To visit the sick.

To bury the dead.

The Beatitudes

1. Blessed are the poor in spirit, for the kingdom of heaven is theirs.

2. Blessed are those who are sad, for they shall be comforted.

3. Blessed are the mild and gentle, for they shall inherit the land.

4. Blessed are those who hunger and thirst for justice, for they shall be filled.

5. Blessed are the merciful, for they shall receive mercy.

6. Blessed are the pure in heart, for they shall see God.

7. Blessed are those who make peace, for they shall be called the children of God.

8. Blessed are those who suffer for my sake, for heaven will be theirs.

The Rosary

The Joyful Mysteries

1. The Coming of Jesus is announced
2. Mary Visits Elizabeth
3. Jesus is Born
4. Jesus is Presented to God
5. Jesus is Found in the Temple

The Sorrowful Mysteries

1. Jesus' Agony in the Garden
2. Jesus is Whipped
3. Jesus is Crowned with Thorns
4. Jesus Carries His Cross
5. Jesus Dies on the Cross

The Glorious Mysteries

1. Jesus Rises from His Tomb
2. Jesus Ascends to Heaven
3. The Holy Spirit Descends
4. Mary is Assumed into Heaven
5. Mary is Crowned in Heaven

Personal Record

Name _____
born _____ in _____

Baptism
Date _____
Priest _____
Parish _____
Godfather _____
Godmother _____

First Communion
Date _____
Priest _____
Parish _____

Confirmation
Date _____
Bishop _____
Parish _____
Sponsor _____
Confirmation name _____

Family Record

Father _____
   born _____ in _____

Mother _____
   born _____ in _____

Brothers and Sisters _____
_____
_____

Father's Family
   Grandfather _____
     born _____
   Grandmother _____
     born _____

Mother's Family
   Grandfather _____
     born _____
   Grandmother _____
     born _____

This is my bed time prayer. . .

This is my own prayer thanking
God for the day. . .

_____

_____

_____

_____

_____

_____

_____

_____

This is my own prayer thanking
God for my friends. . .

_____

_____

_____

_____

_____

_____

_____

_____

_____